Focused Light from a Distant Star

Focused Light from a Distant Star

Poems by

Toni Ortner

© 2023 Toni Ortner. All rights reserved.
This material may not be reproduced in any form, published,
reprinted, recorded, performed, broadcast,
rewritten or redistributed without
the explicit permission of Toni Ortner.
All such actions are strictly prohibited by law.

Cover image by Terry Hauptman
Photographer Coni Richards
Cover design by Shay Culligan

ISBN: 978-1-63980-474-0

Kelsay Books
502 South 1040 East, A-119
American Fork, Utah 84003
Kelsaybooks.com

Acknowledgments

Thank you to the following publications, where versions of these poems previously appeared:

Vermontviews.org: "Creation of the Birds," "Self-Portrait by Frida Kahlo," "IXI," "Gathering Paradise," "Year of the Cicada," "The Savage Sparkler," " The Artist's Wife in the Garden at Skagen," "Join," "59th Street Studio"

Write Action Newsletter: "Dreaming of Her Lover," "In the Library, St. James' Square," "Untitled (Train)," "Portrait of Raul"

The cover is taken from one of the 5' by 40' paintings called *The Songline Scrolls* by the Vermont painter Terry Hauptman. Terry has had extensive national exhibits of her work as well as shows in Vermont. Her global mixed-media scrolls radiate with innovative vision and bridge cultures.

Contents

The Artist's Wife in the Garden at Skagen
    Peder Severin Kroyer   1893
        Oil on canvas   17
The Magpie on the Gallows
    Pieter Bruegel the Elder   1568
        Oil on wood panel   18
Storm at Sea
    Pieter Bruegel the Elder   1568
        Oil on wood panel   19
Dreaming of Her Lover
    George Smith   1868
        Oil on panel   20
In the Library, St. James' Square
    Thomas Pole   1806
        Watercolor   21
Untitled (Train)
    Kiki Smith   1993
        Wax with beads   22
Empanadas (Turnovers)
    Carman Lomas Garza   1991
        Gouache on paper   23
Red Vision
    Leonor Fini   1984
        Oil on canvas   24
Woman with Dog
    Marisol   1964
        Fur, leather, plaster, synthetic polymer, wood   25
Catharsis
    Magdalena Abakanowicz   1985
        Cast bronze   26
Sand Dunes
    Beverly Pepper   1985
        Mylar over wood   27

Marilyn (Vanitas)
  Audrey Flack   1977
  Oil over acrylic on canvas   28
La Bella Dormiente
  Susana Solano   1986
  Iron and lead   29
Creation of the Birds
  Remedios Varo   1958
  Oil on Masonite   30
Portrait of Raul
  Rocio Maldonado   1988
  Oil on canvas   31
Join
  Elizabeth Murray   1980
  Oil on canvas   32
Cape
  Barbara Chase-Riboud   1973
  Multicolored bronze and hemp rope on welded aluminum and steel support   33
King's Heritage
  Anne Truitt   1973
  Painted wood   34
59th Street Studio
  Georgia O'Keeffe   1919
  Oil on canvas   35
Forest British Columbia
  Emily Carr   1932
  Oil on canvas   36
Emily Carr on horseback in the Cariboo, Canada 1904
  photograph   37
Man Among the Redwoods
  Marguerite Thompson Zorach   1912
  Oil on canvas   38

IXI
   Susan Rothenberg   1977
   Flashe and acrylic on canvas   39

Titanic Memorial
   Gertrude Vanderbilt Whitney   1914
   Granite   40

Untitled
   Cindy Sherman   1989
   Color photograph   41

Self-Portrait
   Frida Kahlo   1940
   Oil on canvas   42

Temple, part of India Memory Series
   Howardena Pindell   1984
   Gouache, tempera, postcards, watercolor,
   and acrylic on museum board   43

My Little Effigies
   Annette Messager   1989
   Stuffed dolls, photographs, and grease pencil   44

The Savage Sparkler
   Alice Aycock   1981
   Steel, sheet metal, heating coils, florescent
   lights, motors, and fans   45

Boy
   Jennifer Bartlett   1983
   Oil on canvas   46

Untitled
   Lee Bontecou   1961
   Canvas and welded steel   47

The Year of the Cicada
   Grace Hartigan   1970
   Oil on canvas   48

Self-Portrait
   Leonora Carrington   1936–37
   Oil on canvas   49

Mirror Shadow II
    Louise Nevelson   1985
    Painted wood   50
Linen
    Natalya Goncharova   1912
    Oil on canvas   51
The Blind Leading the Blind
    Louise Bourgeois   1947–49
    Painted wood   52
Natalie Barney   Plate from The Dinner Party
    Judy Chicago   1987
    Chino paint on porcelain   53
Gathering Paradise
    Sandy Skoglund   1991
    Color Cibachrome photograph   54
Fleeing a Dust Storm, Cimarron County,
    Oklahoma
    Arthur Rothstein   1936
    Photogravure printed on a hand-operated
    etching press   55

Preface

Focused Light from A Distant Star was inspired by *Women Artists: An Illustrated History* by Nancy Heller published by Abbeville Press. I studied the photos of art created by women and responded with a poem or a prose poem. The majority of work I responded to was created by women in the last two centuries. The title of each work of art, the artist, the date of creation, and the materials are recorded at the top of each page of the book. The reader can see the art in Nancy Heller's book or on the web.

for Lisa

The Artist's Wife in the Garden at Skagen
Peder Severin Kroyer   1893
Oil on canvas

There she sits absorbed in a book
beneath a white rose bush
petals sprinkled like confetti in her glossy hair
unaware that her husband brush in hand stares.

He dapples the emerald lawn with dark shadows.
He arranges the light so it surrounds her like a halo.

The Magpie on the Gallows
Pieter Bruegel the Elder   1568
Oil on wood panel

Hidden sun
Humid air where white mist gloves gray cliffs
Empty fields with brittle weeds
Black trunks of trees.

A woman in a blue dress with a white hood and a red scarf wrestles with two men.

The wooden gallows tower over the peasants.
A gentleman in white pants and shirt stands hands on hips gazing at the magpie on the gallows.

It is the season of indifference.

Storm at Sea
    Pieter Bruegel the Elder   1568
    Oil on wood panel

There is nothing but the storm and the wild ochre sky.
Eight crazed gulls flung into air.
Clouds layer upon layer.

A faded city in the distance
like a half remembered dream.

The heavy schooner founders in the waves.
We hear the sound of splintered wood and screams.

Dreaming of Her Lover
George Smith   1868
Oil on panel

She bends over an open book
gazes into distance
pen in hand.

She wears a white and gray gown with puffed sleeves
low bodice
rosy alabaster breasts.

Whether her lover is imagined or real
makes no difference.

In the Library, St. James' Square
Thomas Pole   1806
Watercolor

She wears an ivory lace gown with long sleeves
black hair pinned under a rib boned cap
points at a page.

She does not look up from the book to see
the slant of the sun the billowing clouds the ivy.
There is a small silver platter with an untouched cup of tea.

She is definitely sailing here.

Untitled (Train)
Kiki Smith   1993
Wax with beads

I chose the body as a subject because it is the one form we all share.

The heavy naked woman is made of pink wax that looks like flesh.
She bends down to watch the stream of blood
that flows between her legs
puddles on the ground.
Drops of blood trail behind
like the train of a wedding gown.
Whether she is affirming life or letting go we do not know.

It is clear there is no wedding here.
No groom. No little boy in pantaloons.
No diamond ring. No bouquets of white lilies.
No priest. No Bible.
No audience or altar.
No bells that ring from steeples.

The word stigmata comes to mind.

Empanadas (Turnovers)
Carman Lomas Garza   1991
Gouache on paper

The family stands in the kitchen making empanadas.

The grandparents roll out the dough while the son and grandson taste the sugared balls.

There are two little girls their hair tucked under neat white lace caps with white socks and black patent leather shoes with straps.

Laughter   smiles   wooden spoons.

The finished platters are covered with crescent moon-shaped empanadas in the shape of flowers.

The tree of life is painted on the kitchen cabinet.

Red Vision
Leonor Fini   1984
Oil on canvas

Chicago slum
railroad apartment
small rooms
dark green paint peeling off the walls.

You, age six
walking with your baby brother down the narrow hall
to get a drink of water
for your mother who lies in bed delirious with typhoid.

A white skeleton hovers in the air with a malevolent grin
hand raised to snatch.
You scream and jerk your brother back and hold him tight
until the apparition fades from sight.

Pale winter light floods the room.

Woman with Dog
Marisol 1964
Fur, leather, plaster, synthetic polymer, wood

Three women
constructed of artificial materials
painted to look real.

The first has three heads in a neck brace. The head that stares at us has thick red painted lips and dark mascara eyes. The two heads on either side are blind. She wears a tailored bright yellow suit with a black and white patterned skirt. On her head is a shiny plastic fireman's helmet. She poses left foot forward coyly like a model on a runway. Her legs are tattooed in a symmetrical design. She has no arms just a tiny withered right hand over which is draped a narrow leather leash. A white terrier is attached whose ears are raised as if he listens to a tune we cannot hear. He wears a leather collar studded with rhinestones. His body is in a cast so he cannot walk.

The second woman has no head just an orange oval on which is pasted a black and white photo of a nun. This contrasts sharply with the perfect round massive pink breasts that flash like bulbs since she is naked from the waist up.

The viewer starts to get angry right about here.

Catharsis
Magdalena Abakanowicz   1985
Cast bronze

There are 33 pillars cast in bronze
33 the year Christ died.

They stand against a wall in a field of crab grass
olive trees behind   pale blue mountains   white sky

Silent witnesses.

Sand Dunes
Beverly Pepper   1985
Mylar over wood

Temporary installation for the Atlantic Center for the Arts,
New Smyrna Beach, Florida

Under the rising sun
embedded in deep sand
away from the noise of streets and inhabitants of buildings
huge sheets of white Mylar glued to wood
appear
like the broken walls of a fallen temple.

Marilyn (Vanitas)
Audrey Flack   1977
Oil over acrylic on canvas

There she is
  bright smile
    white teeth
      red lips.

She is placed like an ornament on a red draped table. A red candle burns. There is an hourglass the color of blood with sand pouring down. A gold compact with pressed powder is open with a pot of rouge and a slender sable brush. The hands of the watch are stopped at 3:45. We cannot help but wonder if that was the time she died. They said it was suicide. We thought it was murder. Both the Kennedys had been shot along with Martin Luther King and Malcolm X by then, so why would a movie star be different?

We see a red rose in full bloom and a bunch of lush green grapes. There are two ripe pears one green and one yellow ready to be eaten and a blue and white porcelain mug half filled with coffee.

In imagination there is always time left.

La Bella Dormiente
Susana Solano   1986
Iron and lead

A crib should be painted white or blue or pink and made of wood.
This one is iron and lead too heavy to be lifted.
Thick metal bars crisscross the top as if it were a box.
The sides are rusty shields that do not yield.

We cannot leave the spot and stare.
There is no scent of innocent flesh
no talcum powder no blankets no colorful mobiles.

No child or sleeping princess here.

Creation of the Birds
Remedios Varo   1958
Oil on Masonite

Who is to say if a painter creates by the focused light of a distant star
or the notes of a violin running through tubes like chemicals.

The artist appears as a white and brown owl with sharp pointed beak
eyes closed as if dreaming.
The room may be a cell or cave.

She is covered with mottled feathers head to foot but has no wings.
Her elbows are placed squarely on the drafting table
naked dirty feet splayed on an ordinary brown and beige tiled floor.

She wears white kid gloves to hide her claws.

Portrait of Raul
    Rocio Maldonado   1988
    Oil on canvas

Raul leans against the beveled window frame.
He holds a silver sword.

A white stallion prances in the distance
on which an image of him sits.

He wears a yellow flannel night shirt with red fish that fly.
We see shooting stars   magic mushrooms   mussels & crabs
an egg without a shell a flying saucer a smiling skull.
It is a night without moon or music.

He stares as us with pursed lips as if to ask a question.

Join
Elizabeth Murray   1980
Oil on canvas

What God has joined in holy matrimony let no man tear apart.

It seems to be a heart
split in two parts
one red one green.

If the black string is an umbilical cord
then the shape is a fetus not a heart.

What was whole is severed.

The stain is dark and thick as pain.
The space between the two
widens
as we watch.

Cape
    Barbara Chase-Riboud   1973
    Multicolored bronze and hemp rope on welded
    aluminum and steel support

It is not a cape unless cape means to cover.
If so what is hidden is the question.

It looks like braids attached to a headless torso
too massive to be a woman.

Is it a pyramid or priest?

King's Heritage
Anne Truitt   1973
Painted wood

You are dwarfed by a tall wood cross
arms cut too short
to bear His weight.

The wood is painted red like fresh drawn blood
sanded smooth as silk.

Light makes the color run in rivulets.

59th Street Studio
Georgia O'Keeffe   1919
Oil on canvas

Exquisitely Georgia O'Keeffe
no door walls windows floors
no fruits or flowers in a vase
no paints pencils paper
black dominates space
edge hesitates.

Imagine brown asymmetrical shapes
narrow windows covered with cardboard sheets
so she cannot see the light or hear noises from the street.

A crimson arrow points inward.

Forest British Columbia
Emily Carr   1932
Oil on canvas

Frozen in time past cities streets symbols signs
silence envelopes ancient trunks of trees
layer upon layer of sediment and leaves.

In a cave made of black lava
sound echoes into distance.

A sliver of sky hangs like a blue icicle
on a necklace.

Adjectives, nouns and verbs are useless here.
Simile fails.

Emily Carr on horseback in the Cariboo, Canada 1904
photograph

He said, "I cannot understand why a woman would chose to live alone in the wilderness."

Dressed like a man she sits on the stallion
stares expressionless into distance
wears a wide brimmed straw hat to keep off the flies
hundreds of miles from home and barn
no shirts to mend   no socks to darn
no fresh baked bread   no strawberry jam.

Her only friends are the rocks and trees.

Is she humming a tune
Is she dreaming chartreuse?

Man Among the Redwoods
Marguerite Thompson Zorach   1912
Oil on canvas

Bathed in light
a man stands
under trunks of trees
like legs of giants.

The ground is sand.
No streams. Black ravines.

There is a sheer granite cliff he cannot climb
where white vines writhe like serpents.

No return to Eden.

IXI
Susan Rothenberg   1977
Flashe and acrylic on canvas

Larger than life
without saddle bridle rider
the wild horse gallops across the canvas.

Neck outstretched he flashes past like a half remembered image
   from a dream
like the millions of horses that vanished during the Ice Age at the
   end of the Pleistocene.

Hoofs pound dirt to dust
layers of thick red paint laid down like blood or rust.

How we love our Appaloosas Morgans Quarters.
We ride race breed tame.
We live in cities where there once were woods and plains.

The glaciers are melting.
Remember the Eohippus and the Caballine.

Titanic Memorial
Gertrude Vanderbilt Whitney   1914
Granite

Washington Channel Park, Washington, D.C.

He towers over us 18 feet in height
head raised in prayer
arms outstretched
a granite Christ standing on the Book of Life.

A maiden voyage starts with silk brocades and waving flags.
Edward Smith declared, *"I cannot imagine any condition
that would cause a ship to flounder. Modern ship builders
have gone far beyond that."*

Colonial Archibald Gracie said, *"The sea was like glass
and so smooth you could see the stars reflected in it."*

Gone the restaurant where aristocrats sipped champagne.
Gone the ballroom where they danced the night away in frocks.
Divers found a watch stopped at the time the ship went down.
Gone the men who smoked cigars in the billiard room
the boy in white who played croquet
the table covered with silver   linen   lace
the Chinese vases

They sped ahead at 24 knots right into ice.

Untitled
   Cindy Sherman   1989
   Color photograph

A doll has a fixed face.
You change its clothes to alter time and place.
You can be a princess   witch   clown.
You can be a Madonna   maid   whore.

You shift shapes, Cindy.
One image cannot capture who you are.

You pregnant
stare wide-eyed at the camera.

We see a dark navel
huge breasts
gargantuan nipples.

Self-Portrait
Frida Kahlo   1940
Oil on canvas

She glares
high cheekbones brushed with crimson rouge
ebony eyes and hair.

She wears a loose white peasant blouse
a necklace made of thorns wound
tight as a noose around her neck
a blackbird about to rip her throat to shreds.

Compressed by heavy humid air
caged in by dense green leaves and spikes
a pale sky neither day nor night
not a single glimmer of light.

A black cat with yellow eyes is perched like a totem on her shoulder.
Vicious insects flying everywhere.

Is that a white caterpillar or a worm pinned like a jewel above her
   ear?

No laughing monkeys here.

Temple, part of India Memory Series
Howardena Pindell 1984
Gouache, tempera, postcards, watercolor, and acrylic on museum board

Postcards collected from all over the world
sit on the table next to paints and brushes
scenes from India Peru Mexico Japan France
as if memory could be jolted or the dead resurrected
by dragon scales and turrets pinnacles and peaks   birds' wings
    and claws
slatted white strips of fences through which time is hurled
    senseless.

You float in a blue labyrinth.

How to stitch sight to mind without needle or thread
is
the
question.

My Little Effigies
Annette Messager   1989
Stuffed dolls, photographs, and grease pencil

Can betrayal be labeled?
Try 19 stuffed dolls pinned to the canvas titled My Little Effigies.

Grief and loss like shards of glass.
Despair bleeds out the heart.

Make a rag doll of each person.
Lay them down flat as corpses.
Light a match and burn them to a crisp.

Does this make a difference?

The Savage Sparkler
   Alice Aycock   1981
   Steel, sheet metal, heating coils, florescent
   lights, motors, and fans

What kind of machine is this?

We recognize the parts: sheet metal   heating coils   motors   fans.
Florescent strings of lights flash on and off.
There are no switches.
The turbine is huge but does not turn.
There are no signs.
Brown and green look bland
This is not a geometry we understand.

We see what appears to be a wire ladder leading in but no bench on
    which to sit.
No buttons or levers.
Senses reel inside ring after ring of glistening steel.
Trapped in a metal labyrinth without a thread
an increasing sense of dread.

Boy
Jennifer Bartlett   1983
Oil on canvas

Another night in the villa
full moon hung like a lantern
another day of monochrome
when hours stretch like rubber bands about to snap
your only company paints   canvases   brushes.

This is a strange country
whose language you cannot deceiver
all black and blue
cracked swimming pool
tall marsh grass like silver spikes
mist obscuring any trace of light.

The stone statue of the urinating boy by the empty pool
no swimmers no laughter.

You cannot recall what you intended. A joke to imagine what is
    broken can be mended.

Untitled
Lee Bontecou   1961
Canvas and welded steel

The end of days
no glimmer of light
all blacks and grays.

We see
an African woman with asymmetrical breasts
strips of flesh
a man's fist   a severed thigh
the jaw of a dinosaur
sharp teeth like spikes
endless night
all bolts and screws   doors that cannot open
box after box after box
locks without keys
ground without seeds.

The Year of the Cicada
Grace Hartigan   1970
Oil on canvas

It does not matter what you believe
when they come they come
one minute the sky is clear
the next the swarm is here
dark cloud loud sound
buzz of wing snap of jaw
crunching teeth no relief
each leaf devoured down to its stem
no stopping them
they come when they come.

Behind the eight ball the cicada smiles.

Self-Portrait
Leonora Carrington   1936–37
Oil on canvas

Max Ernst is gone

She sits alone in a chair in a room that has no windows or doors.
There is a highly polished floor.
She has been here before.

She wears a green riding jacket.

Bright light saturates.
Heat bears down.

Her childhood rocking horse flies through the air.
She beckons with her hand as if to make the hideous striped hyena
    dance.
Milk leaks from teats she cannot reach.
The pale blue walls do not soothe.

We see a golden canopy and a mural of a running horse.

Love lost cannot easy gallop off.

Mirror Shadow II
Louise Nevelson   1985
Painted wood

Long ago and far away on a bright April day
a mother and daughter walked
through a landscape of wood
black milk cartons   lumber scraps   pieces of doors   alters
hammered together at odd angles.

In and out of boxes   triangles   rectangles
they walked
looking for an arrow to point the way.

Blessed are they who understand
there is no winning hand.

Linen
Natalya Goncharova   1912
Oil on canvas

Before the guests arrive
linen napkins folded into precise triangles and squares
columns and pillars
bowls   bonnet   caps
a tallis with silver threads and tassels
blue shadowed flower petals
stillness folded into rays of blinding light
prisms of white.

As if life were a stage and all you need are the right props.

The Blind Leading the Blind
Louise Bourgeois   1947–49
Painted wood

You did not paint apples   pears   lace.
There are 14 vertical columns hammered to a horizontal frame.
14 severed legs rigid as steel.

Do they strut across the stage?
Does red paint signify rage?
Does black signify grief?

The pillars might be spikes or spears.

When the blind lead the blind
all
is question.

Natalie Barney   Plate from The Dinner Party
Judy Chicago   1987
Chino paint on porcelain

The opal plate honors you
luminescent silver   iridescent blue
ivy petals
entwined in gold vines
your signature symbol.

Fridays at Rue Jacob
surrounded by writers   painters   musicians
ice carved into swans   Italian wines in crystal glasses
canopies on silver trays.
The setting sun lights the chandelier on fire.

You know how to set a scene. You with your blond shimmering hair walking hand in hand with the woman who is your current lover. Are you taking notes in your head as you listen to the guests talk and laugh? Are you waiting for them to leave and dreaming of her breasts? Are you thinking of the book you want to write as the sun goes down and the stars appear?

Critics say the lily is a symbol of the vulva.

On your grave, it says, *"I am this legendary being in which I will live again."*

All breath.
No death.

Gathering Paradise
Sandy Skoglund   1991
Color Cibachrome photograph

Hundreds of black, ugly squirrels made of clay, metal armature, and polyester resin on the floor salute with upraised paws. Others crawl on the walls and hang from ceilings upside down like bats without wings. They creep into every single crack and crevice waving fat tails like flags while the man on the porch sits alone under a beach umbrella blind to the close proximity of flesh and fur bone and claws.

Some clench nuts between their teeth They sniff everywhere.
They bask with delight in the garish pink light.
The door to the pantry is wide open.
The squirrels are indifferent to the man in the chair.

Fleeing a Dust Storm, Cimarron County,
   Oklahoma
Arthur Rothstein   1936
Photogravure printed on a hand-operated
   etching press

Mother begged us not to go, but father said we had no choice and led the way across the roaring field. The reeds snapped like firecrackers. We covered our nose and mouths with wet rags so we could breathe; we spun like leaves. Heads down we tunneled through gusts of dust. Our eyes burned. A thousand hornets stung our skin. We could hear the mare and the filly whinnying in fear their hoofs hitting the walls of the stalls. Wood splintered words. Thick dust burned the barn door. It was worse than a blizzard. Father used an axe. The mare reared and tried to bolt, but father managed to get a rope around her neck and the filly followed head down to the ground.

We took it for granted that what was ours would always be here. There was no warning since the sky was clear.

About the Author

Toni Ortner has had 31 books published; her work has appeared in over 100 literary magazines. She lives in Vermont and gives readings in bookstores and libraries. As Vice President of the nonprofit group Write Action for the last 14 years, she ran the Write Action Radio Hour where she interviewed writers and had them read their work. Her work is in several anthologies, and she has won grants from Pen America and the Author's League. She taught most recently in the English Department at the University of Connecticut.

Her website is where you can view her books and reviews:
toniortner.com

www.ingramcontent.com/pod-product-compliance
Lightning Source LLC
Chambersburg PA
CBHW070942160426
43193CB00011B/1781